PITY THE BATHTUB ITS FORCED EMBRACE
OF THE HUMAN FORM

PITY THE BATHTUB

ITS FORCED

EMBRACE

OF THE

HUMAN FORM

~

POEMS BY

MATTHEA HARVEY

Alice James Books
Farmington, Maine

Library of Congress Cataloging-in-Publication Data

Harvey, Matthea, 1973-
    Pity the bathtub its forced embrace of the human form : poems / by
Matthea Harvey.
        p.cm
    ISBN-13: 978-1-882295-26-5 (pbk.)
    ISBN-10: 1-882295-26-9 (pbk.)
        I. Title.

PS3558.A7193 P58 2000
 811'.6--dc21   00-022222

14 13 12 11 10 9 8 7 6 5

Alice James Books gratefully acknowledges support from the University of
Maine at Farmington and the National Endowment for the Arts.

Alice James Books are published by the Alice James Poetry Cooperative, Inc.,
an affiliate of the University of Maine at Farmington.
Alice James Books
114 Prescott Street
Farmington, Maine 04938

www.alicejamesbooks.org

Cover art: Painting © Ellen Harvey, 1998: The Romantic Bathroom: Bathtub.
Oil on plywood, 13 1/2 x 15 inches.

ACKNOWLEDGEMENTS

Thank you to the editors of the following magazines where these poems first appeared:

Atlanta Review: "The Illuminated Manuscript," "The Need For Consistency"

Boston Review: "Pity the Bathtub Its Forced Embrace of the Human Form," "By Bicycle"

Colorado Review: "Image Cast By a Body Intercepting Light"

Denver Quarterly: "Nude on a Horsehair Sofa by the Sea"

Fence: "The Gem is on Page Sixty-Four," " How All Things Vestigial Gained Prestige"

Grand Street: "Translation"

Iowa Journal of Cultural Studies: "Self-Portraits"

Lit: "In Defense of Our Overgrown Garden"

New England Review: "The Festival of Giovedi Grasso"

The New Republic: "Objective Fatigue"

The North American Review: "Outside the Russian-Turkish Baths"

The Paris Review: "Thermae"

Prairie Schooner: "Frederick Courteney Selous's Letters to His Love"

Seneca Review: "Letting Go"

The Southern Review: "The Oboe Player," "This Holds Water"

Volt: "Paint Your Steps Blue"

Verse: "One Filament Against the Firmament"

Thank you to Alfred A. Knopf, a Division of Random House, Inc. for permission to reprint from *The Man Without Qualities* by Robert Musil.

Many many thanks to my family, friends and teachers.

"In Defense of Our Overgrown Garden" is for Brian.
"Napoleon's Gardens" is for Margarete and David.
"More Sketches for a Beautiful Hat" is for Frances.
"The Gem Is on Page Sixty-Four" is for Sasha.

CONTENTS

Ordinarily, we look at something, and our gaze is like a fine wire or a taut thread with two supports — one being the eye and the other what it sees, and there's some such great support structure for every second that passes; but at this particular second, on the contrary, it is rather as though something painfully sweet were pulling our eye-beams apart.

—Robert Musil, from *The Man Without Qualities*

TRANSLATION

They see a bird that is bright in both beak and feather
And call it cardinal not thinking to import the human
Kind words welcome those who stumble to shore
With the tilt of the sea still in their step salt stains
At their hems that seem to map out coastlines left far
Behind the new songs are the old absurd hopes
A woman wiping the table sings *bring me plans*
And money or fans and honey each word more
Strange yellow flowers spring up in the first lawns
Instead of white dots of daisies how to tell what is
A weed is persistent and is to be emulated says a man
In a tavern in church the preacher lectures on Lazarus
Gesturing wildly as another boatload lurches along
A latitude is a guiding line a platitude a boring line
Chorus the children in school their slates scrawled
And smudged with sums that always seem to come to
Nothing is quite the same here a woman writes a letter
Near the lighthouse but the fog is so thick the words
Run as she writes them for a moment she can't tell
The sea spray from the fog one falls back the other stays
Suspended between two houses in the distance is a
Clothesline with a red shirt on it but she sees a bird

I

Pity the Bathtub Its Forced Embrace of the Human Form

1.

Pity the bathtub that belongs to the queen its feet
Are bronze casts of the former queen's feet its sheen
A sign of fretting is that an inferior stone shows through
Where the marble is worn away with industrious
Polishing the tub does not take long it is tiny some say
Because the queen does not want room for splashing
The maid thinks otherwise she knows the king
Does not grip the queen nightly in his arms there are
Others the queen does not have lovers she obeys
Her mother once told her *your ancestry is your only*
Support then is what she gets in the bathtub she floats
Never holds her nose and goes under not because
She might sink but because she knows to keep her ears
Above water she smiles at the circle of courtiers below
Her feet are kicking against walls which cannot give
Satisfaction at best is to manage to stay clean

2.

Pity the bathtub its forced embrace of the whims of
One man loves but is not loved in return by the object
Of his affection there is little to tell of his profession
There is more for it is because he works with glass
That he thinks things are clear (he loves) and adjustable
(she does not love) he knows how to take something
Small and hard and hot and make room for
His breath quickens at night as he dreams of her he wants
To create a present unlike any other and because he cannot
Hold her he designs something that can a bathtub of
Glass shimmers red when it is hot he pours it into the mold
In a rush of passion only as it begins to cool does it reflect
His foolishness enrages him he throws off his clothes meaning

To jump in and lie there but it is still too hot and his feet propel
Him forward he runs from one end to the other then falls
To the floor blisters begin to swell on his soft feet he watches
His pain harden into a pretty pattern on the bottom of the bath

3.
Pity the bathtub its forced embrace of the human
Form may define external appearance but there is room
For improvement within try a soap dish that allows for
Slippage is inevitable as is difference in the size of
The subject may hoard his or her bubbles at different
Ends of the bathtub may grasp the sponge tightly or
Loosely it may be assumed that eventually everyone gets in
The bath has a place in our lives and our place is
Within it we have control of how much hot how much cold
What to pour in how long we want to stay when to
Return is inevitable because we need something
To define ourselves against even if we know that
Whenever we want we can pull the plug and get out
Which is not the case with our own tighter confinement
Inside the body oh pity the bathtub but pity us too

Nude on a Horsehair Sofa by the Sea

I don't know what to do with his body.
It looks smooth — & heavy too —
from the way the sofa's mahogany claws
sink into the sand. Every other wave
is brown, the ones in between a light liquor
bottle green, & the strip of wet sand
the froth laps, then leaves, is glass-
brown & shouldn't act like mud
but does. When a seagull struts by
I see the others flick their brushes
in irritation over that spot as if to
drive it away — & me, I'm avoiding
the subject, still fretting over how to paint
the word *sometimes* because the pebbles
only show when the water's had a chance
to settle. I can tell he's secretly moving
his toes along the grain of the sofa
& back, so the hairs lie smooth, then
bristle as one wave crests & another
crashes. The woman next to me sighs.
Her clouds look like dark whales floating
in the sky, her brush hovers over
them then dips down to make
an awkward dab at the spot between
the model's thighs. It is starting
to drizzle now & each wave has a pocked
& peaked landscape of its own & people
are folding their easels & shielding
their paintings with their bodies as they run
to the striped cabanas. Perhaps he will whisk
out a cloak & wade slowly into the water,
silk billowing about his fine white ankles.

Perhaps he has to help carry the sofa. I turn
and trudge after the others, picking a path
through the driftwood littered like collarbones
on the beach. I want a way to take it all
with me — the sag of the sofa beneath him &
the curve of the ocean which is what I think
the iris must look like from inside the eye.

THIS HOLDS WATER

Those who have no visitors visit the outside weather permitting
them to sit in a row on deckchairs all wearing the same lipstick
Lilac Luxury age and an inattentive nurse conspiring to lend them
matching complexions *my husband worked on the locks* says
the woman farthest from the door the other women nod
on cue reach into the pockets of their housedresses for their letters
which with the help of a magnifying glass she reads out loud
to them this is the most important moment of the week listening to her
judgments on this niece's penmanship that grandson's goals
choice of paper type of envelope they all know she embellishes
the letters always have more declarations of love than
when someone else reads them they know in advance
that a postcard never wins that a wedding announcement is stiff
competition but they still wait anxiously for her
admiring smile her hands weighing the letter and its contents
then announcing *this holds water* the highest compliment
as it is what her husband said after repairing a lock that was letting
the boats down too quickly a volunteer comes out to collect
their cups of weak tea she quips *this holds more water*
than it oughta and they all smile at his confusion
knowing why she looks at him adoringly as he lowers
her into the wheelchair she is remembering lying on the bank
of a canal in the sun watching him work the levers of the lock
until the boat reaches a lower level and floats down the river

A fragment of speech cuts through the thick night air —
    How dare you? mutters a young man on the steps
to the older man beside him. Gone the shared shedding of
    clothes. Gone the clang of lockers, slow slipping into
the pool of shallow water, legs lolling, warm tiles. He looks
    pleased to see color and assumptions drain from
his companion's face. A child surveys the street for a lost toy,
    goes inside the slamming door, two stories up a stereo
shuts off as a young woman settles to sleep, a siren spirals
    away down Second Avenue and it is quiet. The two men
now standing in anytime, anyplace. The older man's confusion
    becomes wonder, the younger's malice, delight, they are master
and apprentice, it is Venice, they have finally discovered how
    to take all the color out of glass and make it clear, they,
who have seen the dull red of a lover's cheek as it turns away from
    sleep towards morning, the dense green of a forest encircling
a mountain, a room speckled blue by sunlight as it filters through
    a vase, have spent a lifetime wanting to take it all away.
Impossible to tell what is loss, what is gain. Impossible to know
    what warrants celebration. The stained glass windows
still sparkle with saints and miracles, but the man who made them
    carried slivers of glass in his fingers until the day he died —
some days feeling blessed by their glistening, other days
    raging at not being able to press his wife's hand in his.
Streetlights come on. One man looks longingly at the damp curl
    his fingers have been told not to touch, the other scans
the street for a taxi. Neither notices the steam that swells up
    from the bath's underskirts and mixes with the fog.

Self Portraits (After Paintings by Max Beckmann)

Double Portrait, Carnival, 1925

I worked on us
for weeks. Painted my face, then yours. I loved yours,
made it smile as our doubles struck silly poses.
Me the hapless clown, you both general and horse —
the fore-legs your legs, the hind legs, horse,
high heels mimicking hooves. I gave you a huge hat,
a soft grey jacket, a white cravat, closed your fingers
around the reins. And for myself? I painted a cigarette,
a purple suit and shiftless feet. I thought I was painting you
a poem of color, of spotted horses and orange cuffs.
But the horse had a wild eye, the tent flap gaped,
and we stood there in disguise.

Self-Portrait in Tuxedo, 1927

I can mock the debonair pose of hand on hip,
casual grip of cigarette stub, but I only masked the body.
It was the one time I asked myself, truly,
what face I saw in the mirror, then answered
with a storm of brushstrokes on my forehead,
a shadow lapping my eye with its dark tongue,
misery marking my mouth. One is not the same
after such clarity. You liked my stance. Said if I
were a stranger leaning on a wall at a party you would
ask me to dance, would rashly press against me.
I did not point out the small glowing ash. After all,
in a dream sequence your taffeta would not burn.

SELF-PORTRAIT WITH GLASS BALL, 1936

And so I held it softly to my chest,
firmly, but with no fear of it breaking
for this is how it is with things we take for granted.
I did not look down, thinking I knew what was reflected there;
myself — only more so, as in a lover's eyes.
What do I see there now?
The richest colors. Glimmers of you
which I painted quickly, cradled heedlessly,
spending hours instead creasing my forehead
into a set of elegant birdwings, angling the door
onto blackness so the future could darken my eyes.
And that mouth. Strange that gripping a brush with determination
can produce such resignation. If only I had looked
into that third eye — for though it had no ties to visions
it knew my heart, was my heart.

SELF-PORTRAIT YELLOW-PINK, 1943

I said goodnight with yellow on my cheek,
and in the morning you woke laughing
to tell me of a dream where I hired ten numskulls
to work on the garden who painted all the elms
in gold filigree. You wanted me to put the glittering trees
in the picture but I had to disagree. It was your dream,
not mine, though it crept in. I painted myself
as the man you might have met in sleep — his arms hugged
to his chest protectively, as if you or your dream
had rested there, invisible, a near-dimple by the mouth,
a shadow of a sleeping cap which wasn't on his head.
You pouted and asked for trees.
Sometimes you are very hard to please.

SELF-PORTRAIT WITH BLUE-BLACK GLOVES, 1948

Is it true that the night you said to me, sweetly,
mischievously, *your hands are like large flat fish
that fill my rivers*, I climbed out of bed and began to paint
those gloves? I do not think I meant it cruelly. I remember
feeling suddenly small, leaving the bed to sit squarely
first in front of the mirror, then the canvas, and then,
taking a thick brush, painting myself larger.
In the dark my hands, forearms and forehead
gleamed white, and it seemed right to cover at least
fingertip to wrist. But I see what you see.
You woke to sunrise alone and found me
asleep in front of my own stripe of orange,
a grim look in the eyes on the canvas that frightened you.
How to explain why I crawled away like a cricket
to sing my song in a corner, knowing you
would not find it beautiful.

SELF-PORTRAIT IN BLUE JACKET, 1950

What is not in the picture: a field of poppies,
morning glories clinging to their vine in a rainstorm,
images that would not yield their meaning when I picked up
the brush. I once told myself not to rush such things,
then found their lush colors gone. One consolation:
lost money that goes through the wash is still money
when it reappears. So I paid for the colors' brightness
with crumpled bits of memory, and though I was the subject
again, there were unpaintable moods in the blues
of my coat, electric green seas curled in the chair's arm.
It was bigger than me. The perspective was not mine.
I hid my mouth with a cigarette and long fingers,
wiped the brushes dry and called for you to look at him
still holding my breath.

ORNAMENTAL

Winters, he reletters
the sign on the mailbox in gold
paint. The old grooves mean there
is no need for reshaping, he's just filling in,
biding time. In autumn, he drains the fountain,
wipes the stone fishes' mouths clear of calcium
and algae, puts the Japanese carp in a tank. Summers
they come up to suck his fingers, their orange mouths
gaping as if to swallow the sun, finding no sustenance,
but perhaps some comfort in the simplicity of his offering.
A child will do the same as its teeth prepare to come in. He
must have done it once though he cannot remember. He does
not like break-throughs, is happier controlling boundaries,
resisting the inevitable. This is spring's work: resting the
ladder against branches which hold his weight and do not
give. Some sprigs of green grow as they should, do not
need trimming. Others resist the patterns he imposes —
horsehead, cone, chesspiece, rooster — choosing their
own unruly designs instead. He takes the shears
to such rebellion. All summer he snips and
supervises. And finally, one day a tree
acquiesces, crying, *not just maple,*
red sugar maple! He crows with
delight as the rooster
turns red.

II

PAINT YOUR STEPS BLUE

It is spring & people are out repainting their front steps
Glacier blue because this village is closer to the glacier than
The volcano emits a tiny rumble & drools lava once every few
Years go by & its followers grow fat with having nothing to
Fear here is of the icy-&-slowly-approaching variety
Babies turn their screams inside out & slowly turn
Blue paint is supposed to fool the glacier into thinking
It has been where it hasn't though some think the command
Meant footsteps so crevasse explorers paint those blue too
As per the thread in the Labyrinth it helps you find the way
Back in the Time Of Much Sun so many layers melted away
That the Flower Layer emerged & people picnicked on
The meadow had been swallowed whole many millennia
Before it had been a pink & yellow stripe on the glacier's side
Like a layer of jam & custard in a poundcake now through
The ice they saw details meadowsweets silver pussytoes &
Thyme seemed like an appropriate thing to be trapped in
There was a girl who loved the meadow so much that one night
She strapped on her skates & dared to skate on its surface
The story goes that one of her blades cut through the ice &
Nicked one of the pussytoes suddenly all the air smelled incredibly
Sweet & the glacier roared moved forward & cut the village in
Half their ancestors were in a layer that they had given no name
To understand why the portrait painter was fed to the glacier after
He painted it down to the tiniest detail one would have to know
That they had been punished before & they were sure that
Including the Lava Layer would not be well-received indeed
It was the reason some of them had succumbed to doubt & left
The village is getting ready for calving already bits of the glacier
Are breaking off & floating out to sea one woman does not like
To watch it is not so long since her own daughter left her she goes
Inside she picks up her daughter's picture of course it is white

With just a hint of the human everything here is overexposed
She hears the familiar sound of paint being slapped onto stone
& the delighted screams of the children in the schoolyard as they
Lie on the ground & a boy on a skateboard rides over them

Because it means looking into the sun, people can barely see
    the two boys in the belltower or the two cables running
from it to the ground. One boy crouches in a boat without oars,
    the other hangs from a harness in the next archway over,
ready to jump. He doesn't have wings, but he is cherubic, picked
    for his wide eyes and smooth cheeks. As he falls he holds
the bouquet the way he's been told to — far out in front of him
    so it looks like a message from God. And in case
the image isn't enough, there's the boy in the boat, tossing
    interpretation into the crowds. If the boat wobbles instead
of gliding, it's because he has to get the last few pamphlets
    and poems out from under his feet. No gold unless
the gondola is empty when he lands. He is lucky. It is windy
    and the words go far. Together their descents form
two arms of a compass. Between them, as if they had drawn it,
    the piazza. Must it mean something if two boys who fall
from the same spot land in opposite corners? Must there always
    be a lesson? To me it looks like a diagram of the distance
between what we believe and what we do, but it doesn't hold
    my attention. The crowd is cheering as the boat's bottom
scrapes along the stones; the other boy is handing over
    his flowers even before his heels hit the ground.
Dogs are leaping around the fountain with poems in their mouths
    and the sun slips down the churchsteps one by one.

By Bicycle

It's not good or bad it's how you get around these
Tiny hedged-in lanes that criss-cross town
Maneuverable only by bicycle because the larger
Roads are for sheep and cows who have to move
Together is a brief season when there are two ruts
In the mud instead of one but rain romancing always
Leads to rust and that of course leads to one place only
Hope there isn't a waiting list and a reprimand
Waiting when you arrive at the repair shop smile
And speak quietly and give your explanation
It is not a place for banter go to the barber
These men were all once like the boy I knew
Would end up here when I watched him
Run the bicycle chain along his chin to see
How it felt bumpy he said I said you have grease
On your chin fooled around with a shuttlecock and left
It at that   he doesn't recognise me turns away
Murmuring to enter the back room to enter
The back room is every non-apprentice's dream
No facts but lots of rumors that the vicar has the firstborn
Lamb shorn to pad his seat that Mrs. Stavely once slashed
Her own tires in a fit of pique which is why she doesn't
Have one now she walks with a cane and is a lesson
To us all this is possible but what of the stories about
That room and the bicycles upside down on benches
And those men with the clear eyes and hands in their pockets
Singing and the spokes all spinning in response

How wonderful to have something felt be fact, to be told you cannot
    go on for one minute more, thinks the woman watching
the trees casting spotted shadows on the front lawn of the guest house.
    Across the street a narrow-hipped nun slips inside a glass door —
the reflected clouds bounce on its surface for a moment, then stick,
    looking halted there as if they wanted to follow her in.
The woman is trying not to look at the two naked girls on the balcony
    next to hers who looked up when she first appeared, then lay
their heads back down. Only a woman. She could hear them think it
    as they shifted. She squints at a square in the book on her lap,
studies the old diagram again: the hand is in a kind of harness,
    immobilized so only the middle finger works, lifting and
lowering a small triangular weight. Between finger and weight a stylus
    copies the decreasing arcs onto paper. She likes imagining
the scientists setting their tiny traps for fatigue and lying in wait, likes
    that only the hand is pictured; no face pantomimes what has just
been proven. Just once she would like to feel that certainty on her tongue,
    to turn to someone and say this is what you have done.

THE NEED FOR CONSISTENCY

Once the stagecoach was stopped & the thieves found
Nothing could have pleased him more for
He had been there all the time with his pinstripes
Perfectly aligned with those of the coach's interior
His hands & head hidden behind a pair of matching
Cushions were crucial he concluded from this outing
& henceforth left the houndstooth stagecoach in the
Stable because its cushions had tassels which didn't blend
In general when he was irritated he would play with his
Chameleon putting her on a paisley pillow or a tartan
Scarf & then scolding her fiercely for being so quick
To change himself to match the world would have been
Weak & he thought his reversal put him on par with
The gods watched in amusement as he ordered the park
Mowed to match his socks & the lake dyed to offset
His tie because of course his was another life skewed by
Misunderstanding as his father's final words to his mother
Before he left had been *This porridge has the most terrible*
Consistency became his crusade then as a way to side
With his mother but when he looked in the dictionary
His eyes were still blurry & he missed definition number
One day she almost asked him why he demanded spinach
When wearing his school uniform & milk with blueberries
Mashed in it when he had on his pajamas & why he wanted
A twin but she supposed missing his father made him act
Strange stories circulated about his relationships with
Women whispered that he was apparently impervious to
Sudden fits of tears unpredictable pouting or other forms of
Flirting & the woman he married only realized later that
Patching her tin roof in a silver jacket had lured him
To her painting the basemolding a dark brown so her
Dachshund wouldn't stand out seemed silly but the dog

Liked it because his barks got better reactions & it was
Easier to sneak up on the servants & steal bits of their
Dinner was always served at seven & though she hid her
Lovers in cupboards & made them tiptoe past the trellises
They never lasted long because they soon realized she
Was feigning fright just to keep them interested & that
She knew exactly what time her husband would be back

FREDERICK COURTENEY SELOUS'S LETTERS TO HIS LOVE

1.

Why do you not ask me about the lions you write of the dying
willow in the garden detailing its species as *lustgarten weeping*
and neglect to say if you miss me at all though I think perhaps
that is what you mean to say you cannot imagine it here
my tent floor is a meadow of animal skins my own silky and papery
from wind and sun and sometimes I think the color of my eyes
will have to dull to let in all this brightness dull in the way glass
fades after years and years in the sea last night I saw a lion yawn
so hugely it swallowed the orange sun and then with one bullet
I blew the last bit of its breath away and crossed the desert to its side
and held it in my arms still warm it is so strange to be surrounded
by animals larger and greater than me and watch them fall to their knees
still shuddering with that last longing for life and now I have
its tawny pelt beside me its hair two shades lighter than yours
and rougher you would love the flamingoes here skinny and pink
as hairbands they only appear when there's water speaking of which
I am drinking the tea you sent without sugar it is so bitter
I cut the package open with the same knife that slit three throats today
and I am sorry but I don't know when I'm coming back because lonely
as I am I wake most mornings thinking I cannot leave this

2.

Each leaf that falls leaves a scar is a strange thing to write
about a tree but thank you for your letter don't worry
I think your handwriting is pretty only a bit cramped it has the look
of someone stuck in a living room surrounded by knick-knacks
and patterned wallpaper which you are does mine look wider
since I came here I think it must because there's nothing
to close me in except this forest of the fierce and fast and willowy
which I am felling one by one the giraffes crumple so quickly
perhaps you should chop down your tree it seems to pain you so

this morning was sweltering and I longed to hear your cool voice
mine has gone wild from lack of company or containment
the wind treats it like any other cry of territory sending it the way
of the vultures who follow me for what I leave behind I imagine
my table manners have been left somewhere as I have no table
and the smell of fresh meat over a fire makes my mouth water
so I eat as quickly as the lions less savagely I suppose there is beauty
in the way their jaws smack around red meat and by the end of the day
the carcass is neatly stripped anyway the manners of the desert
are different and I am learning would you have me unlearn them

3.
It is not as if I hadn't already told you that we have been killing
only what we need is a perfect specimen of each species
so when I see a crowd of antelope prance by I mentally strip the fur
from their heads picturing the skulls skinless in my collection
the hooves arranged in first position ballet style on my makeshift shelf
next to my notes and your letters only three of those so far the lions
are the only trouble there is the rule that whoever draws first blood
gets the skin so though I have finished off in the hundreds my catch
is in the tens I am learning to be less judicious think less shoot more
my shoulder aches a little from the gun's recoil it springs back the way
you did when I brought you that first dead offering such things
are natural how does your cat show its devotion after all he seems
like a hothouse flower when I think of him now fenced in and coddled
with saucers of milk imagine the ivory here the tusks like thick cream
sometimes as much as sixty smooth inches of it if you count the curve
while the elephant's skin is so impervious and wrinkled that nothing
disturbs it not even the touch of a butterfly I find them maddening
with all their fluttering in sunny spots teasing me with velveteen wings
and fancy markings such flirtation I chase them on my days off

4.

I've killed one pride only to have another replace it
if I leave this place someone will replace me I hate leaving
the skins at the dock for the trip to the continent seeing them folded
into boxes tissue paper stuffed between the teeth and around the snout
they are headed for fancy living rooms like yours but maybe
you envy the dead their present bedfellow and wouldn't want one
on your floor am I right to mention this I do think about home
it's just the thought of being cooped up in a ship again surrounded
by crates if only I could keep the lions unpacked spread around me
like a version of Noah and his twos Jesus and his flock
certainly these lions have never sailed before why should they
be cargo perhaps they would spring to life in the sea air the males
lolling about on deck their manes matted with salt the females
foraging in the dark waves for fish such fantasies you will say
but why should I go home when there is nothing for me
to do but plan my next trip and by the time I came back here
I would have missed the moment when the young elephant
I've been watching discovered his trunk right now silly creature
he still uses his mouth when he would learn so quickly
if he kept it closed sometimes I feel like that
did you get my last letter will you get this one and reply

5.

I dreamt of you last night furiously stamping on a piece of dark
metal that was to become my ship and when you saw me watching
you shot me a look that was even darker it is not like you
not to write back right away I started another letter that began
there is someone else isn't there I don't blame you if it is true
that this is why you have stopped writing but then I tore that one up
and here I am wondering if the ships have started sailing more slowly
I am trying to latch my heart to the sun's slow ascent and not let it beat

with this insinuating anxiety I am quick in my conclusions often wrong
perhaps there is no one as you know there is no one for me but you
must understand my absence counts for so little in England
while my presence here is felt tenfold by creature and creator
alike as they seem in this place of extremes it is night now
and the scuttlings and calls have dwindled to the occasional scream
as a night hunter swoops out of the darkness with death in its mouth
for the moment they are safe from me in their burrows and nests
the patterns of their skins melting into the shadows but tomorrow
one of you will have to step out from the cover of silence and face me

6.
Have you made a flimsy necklace to trail around your pale neck
out of the stamps I gave you before I left did you let them dry out
curl up at the edges and lose their adhesive you have not stuck
by me not even in this small task of paper pen and ink I shall keep on
writing is the only link I have to you and it is weaker now one-sided
like the lion who roars to the dunes and grasses around him getting no
answer but the frightened silence of prey who pray to never be close
enough to have to answer with their flesh enclosed please find
tooth of muskrat smear of vulture liver rhinoceros horn
zebra whiskers one black one white see how your name
is inscribed in losses across this plain as I mourn the animals mourn too
knowing I am losing my mind over losing you and knowing also
how I shall measure my pain against their hides and tomorrows
my old memories are drying up the new ones are more suited
to this climate light and granular as they drift across my mind
resisting attachment the one I remember is the childhood story I told
you about the ice cracking under me when I was skating and me lying
down and drifting on one slab as the others disappeared into the water

7.

I once saw my life through the lens of one of your amber earrings
saw tiny skeletons caught in the silver oval with no chance
of struggling free and felt trapped and suffused with all
the sweetness and stickiness of your affection here surrounded
as I am by such spectrums of color and life suddenly all is clear
here I am the trapper littering the landscape with corpses
no longer feeling as if the path of my life is being cut into rock
by passion's aimless meanderings I look back to you as though
through a telescope in this I mean I know what I want now
are the hidden things the intangible and unimaginable all
that you spoke of long ago I thought it was all about the chase
I reveled in hardships practicing sleeping on the dormitory floor
for when I would have the ground as my bed but I never practiced
sleeping with my knees in the hollow of another's knees or breathing
slowly together instead I learnt the shallow breath of one who must
always remain undetected and in this way I have let my face slip from
your dreams I am here I am combing the grasses for hidden lions
riding after herds of elephants coming home with my own skin torn
my disguises and ploys seen for what they are by simple animals
who turn around and charge when they have been betrayed

III

In Defense of Our Overgrown Garden

Last night the apple trees shook and gave each lettuce a heart
Six hard red apples broke through the greenhouse glass and
Landed in the middle of those ever-so-slightly green leaves
That seem no mix of seeds and soil but of pastels and light and
Chalk x's mark our oaks that are supposed to be cut down
I've seen the neighbors frown when they look over the fence
And see our espalier pear trees bowing out of shape I did like that
They looked like candelabras against the wall but what's the sense
In swooning over pruning I said as much to Mrs. Jones and I swear
She threw her cane at me and walked off down the street without
It has always puzzled me that people coo over bonsai trees when
You can squint your eyes and shrink anything without much of
A struggle ensued with some starlings and the strawberry nets
So after untangling the two I took the nets off and watched birds
With red beaks fly by all morning at the window I reread your letter
About how the castles you flew over made crenellated shadows on
The water in the rainbarrel has overflowed and made a small swamp
I think the potatoes might turn out slightly damp don't worry
If there is no fog on the day you come home I will build a bonfire
So the smoke will make the cedars look the way you like them
To close I'm sorry there won't be any salad and I love you

Again housewives took blue pills to magnify the moment
When they rounded the curve of a chocolate cake &
Were about to find out whether the frosting would
Last year when something truly predictable happened
People quit Planners Anonymous in droves & a
Certain amount of I-told-you-so-ing went on at the
Dissenters' Sewing Circle whose members stitched
Certainty into their samplers & delighted in homespun
Advice was dispensed officially by the Probability Channel
Which claimed to be the only thing you could count
On the tenth anniversary of uncertainty they generated
Thousands of new probability curves which were then
Reflected in fads voluptuous women were fully in fashion
Since unlike muscles their curves were quirky & God-
Given the unusually low chance of chandeliers killing
A relative all heirs & heiresses had them hung in their
Living rooms & then sat on their satin sofas hopefully
Waiting was slang for adolescence its symptoms were
So revered special footstools with gold fringe were placed
By the phone when the first signs of sulking surfaced
Purpose was scorned in all but the very old who were
Also idolized because the anticipation of death made their
Minds wander & meant their sandwiches always lacked
Something went wrong with the lottery & someone won
Though the government claimed it was one of a series of
Tests in school were rarely given but frequently announced
Then pulses taken & palms ranked according to sweat
No Reason To Fret was a swear as was Don't Worry About
It hurt the governor's ratings a bit when he punished the
Unflappable Flappers for a rather predetermined performance
At the capitol ball but the party line was that he was playing
With notions of complacency & that they'd all soon be

Surprised which sent the people into a series of speculative
Flurries were given a 12% probability rating & in the
Supermarket parking lot a man who fainted on his Ford
When a receipt & a tissue flew by on the wind was given
A medal which he modestly said he had never expected

MEMENTO MORI

1.
a brown leaf struggles against the sky
above it the leaves are gone below they are beginning
to fall a crow approaches claws curling as it lands
on the branch and the small tree shudders branches bowing
weight weight but the leaf is already falling
tiny skeleton arching against the updraft collapsing
back into itself then the final spiral of signature
again the crow it has seen something on
the doorstep glint of silver foil I do not think it is
like other birds dipping its beak in the milk
this one wants the lid off wants to give the sun
its chance to change things when the mother comes out
to collect the bottles the cream on top of this one
has already begun to curdle and thicken the children
their small shoulders hunched with sleep will not drink it
she spoons the lumps into her coffee saying *look
rosettes of cream* but they are not interested in her
faded roses do not see her sudden gesture as they grab
another bottle rip off the lid and drink it down

2.
the actor tips forward on his toes as if the words were
strung on a string just inches before him if he would just
begin just open his mouth when his heels hit the stage
the prompter speaks *at what risk* and he starts the monologue
his tongue suddenly slick with remembering she leans her head
against the velvet curtains keeps the script open her finger
following his progress from her perch she predicts
he will get stuck during the sofa scene it's in his clenched
fists the slight tilt of the neck the body saying *do I remember*
as the mind hurries forward he would do well as the angel

in a play she once saw hovering in a harness singing strange
unearthly songs some people do not belong to their bodies
she hears it in his voice the smoother slightly higher tone
of the rehearsed words the gravelly register of *oh fuck*
when he trips on a tarp she tries to be unobtrusive so he
will not depend on her but marks his mistakes
in soft lead pencil the script shines where she is needed

3.
she scans the air around their heads for puffs of breath
as she drives by they are so still their matted fur
sunken between outposts of bone the corn stubble
black and gold where it shows through the snow
she has watched cows in summer seen their noses
dry up and crack like mud puddles in the sun
the swishing tail seeming to guide rather than scold
the flies when there is only green before them
do they know what is coming these months
of blinding snow nostrils plugged with circles
of ice they don't turn their backs on it or huddle together
and then the cows are behind a hill now a few miles back
small towns interrupt the road with their slower speed limits
it gets darker there is an abandoned power station
ahead she sees the row of pylons leading away from here
the wires sagging between them how the sky dark blue at its top
turns green then yellow-brown where it hits the ground

4.
footprints in the flour what looks like a concrete mixer
hums in the corner and a man bent over looks inside
its mouth watching a ball of batter tumble back
and forth at first it is surprisingly elastic leaving

beige threads on the sides of the machine then slowly
it begins to cohere almost every stage is here bowls covered
with cloth sourdough starter starting to lose its sweetness
dough dented with fingerprints greased tins the finished
loaves in a pile on the table only the baking is hidden
he does not believe in oven lights or poking the bread
with a metal prong to see what sticks he will come back
in an hour any customer who comes in will find himself
alone in this room everywhere the scent of yeast rising
there is a notepad to mark what they have taken
a metal tin for money later he will look inside it
as always on purpose they have left too much

THE OBOE PLAYER

His lips are full, but to play he must fold them in,
make a tight line of those wet curves. It is shocking to see
them sprout out again when he finishes playing a long note,
takes a breath. The sound he produces is never thin enough,
cannot express *I am a lost nymph in the woods* without adding,
a voluptuous nymph at that. He has tried to take the wink
out of his playing, read the most obscure books on the subject,
one filled with circus metaphors: *think tightrope*
but he is always down in the sawdust, slapping a seal,
pinching the plump curves of an acrobat. The audience loves
or hates him; there is no in-between. Those who pick
at their programs wish his solo were over, others look down
thinking he would only have to look at a bundle of green twine
and it would burst into flower. Both flute and clarinet
become breathless in their attempts to outdo him.
The conductor who approached the podium resolving
to rein him in abandons his brisk baton strokes, succumbs
to swaying. And the oboist, who has been whispering
his sins into that dark wooden tube hoping for absolution,
flinches as the house lights come up hearing *want*
echoed back in each footstamp, each clap.

Napoleon's Gardens

We were betting all yellow
for the day of arrival. That trip
we had a lemon tree on board
laden with half-ripe fruit.
How I cursed you when a storm
hit & in the middle of waves
& wind I was stuck cupping
the lemons in my hands
so they wouldn't fall off.
The next day I was the one
who wiped the salt from
its leaves lest they wrinkle
or develop an unsightly glaze.
I dare say there was no one
on that island who would have
told you *grow it from seed*
but risk my life for a lemon?
When we got rosebushes
for passengers, I took one look
at their prickles & assigned them
to cargo: deck privileges only
on fair days. Besides, it made us
soft to have them on board,
all pink & white like a row
of pretty girls soaking up sun.
I could swear they were flirting.
With the tree it was different.
Like us it sickened of saltwater,
longed for land. Understand then,
why when I saw St. Helena I changed
the logbook from ten lemons to nine.
We needed to taste what you tasted.

How All Things Vestigial Gained Prestige

A man once sent his daughter to Show & Tell with
An old scroll that listed what was delicious & what was
Not only did it move soil into the former category
& peanut butter into the latter but people immediately
Made soil sandwiches assuming that the paper was
Real documents of this sort came along rarely
& for this generation the Dew Claws Clause was
It was found in an old law book which had a creak
In its spine that was tested & shown to be authentic
The unusual ruling stated *the court hereby declares that*
In the case of Miss. Fleur vs. The State the defendant
Is granted universal admiration as per the vestiges of her
Loveliness is to be honored regardless of its lessening
Appendix X shows her nose prior to the incident
With the parasol & a file photo shows her days later
At the mall with a court escort enforcing the judge's
Order disintegrated as the news spread & both
Political parties had to pretend to be pleased as
Depending on how one interpreted the footnote
It could mean change or a return to how things had been
Before long hairier men experienced an increase in
Propositions from women in bars & the subway reported
It would investigate new tail-space for those who still
Felt a certain rapport with their rudimentary vertebrae
Though frogs became extinct the leaders said it was
Nothing the farmers tried would dissuade their flocks
Of sheep from stealing away and slipping into the sea

MORE SKETCHES FOR A BEAUTIFUL HAT

Plain Black Hat with Waterfall Veil
for the widow in extravagant mourning.
Clear-Stream Cloche with matching
transparent galoshes. Other accessories
necessary: blue & green fish clips
to secure the hair, pebble polish for the toes.
Rain-Glazed Slate Roof Hat —
dark shimmery crepe cut into
rough & overlapping rectangles,
patches of moss stitched on in green
& yellow thread (comes with puns
included — liking lichen, mind
in the gutter...) Of course actual
tiny tin gutters would be gauche,
pathetically mimetic. Equally
regrettable: those aigrettes made of
birdwings. I like a challenge & fashion
my feathers out of horsehair, fur & wire.
There's the Tidepool Pillbox — by all
accounts ordinary until you tilt your head
& sloshing is heard. Guaranteed
to make the lover linger. Or Upstream
Requiem: straw toque dyed dark blue
with a tangerine ribbon around the brim
& a velvet cloak lined with large silk salmon
that flash when you stalk from the room.
I don't presume to say you'll be leaving
anyone anytime soon, but when I heard
he was beginning to drown in debt it was
naturally quite an inspiration to me.

Minarets & Pinnacles

Around 5 o'clock even the grounded crowds
of aging coquettes who still believed the bat of an eyelash

or two could cause the miracle of upward mobility,
stood still, watching the tangerine streaks of sunset.

They did not remember why they did it.
Ties to God had proven fickle — first the prayermats

were put in the pantry in case the maid happened to upset
the olive oil & then the gold podiums seemed perfect

for those lengthy articles about real estate & roof repairs.
At night, tucked in their towers, they dreamt of falling,

like most people do, but though they'd been told the tale
of Babel, their situation was admittedly different:

this was each man & his minaret. Capitalism on the up
& up. Pinnacles of success moved from the hypothetical

to the real: now you picked your peak & started climbing.
Naturally it was getting harder & harder to find

an available & presentable mosque — smaller conical
structures called Mini-Minarets were being successfully marketed.

Members of the upper class, cramped on their sagging balconies,
cast cynical smiles at their new neighbors. They liked to

languidly take out their lorgnettes & study the wet patches
under the upstarts' armpits & their awful freckles

while feasting on roast duck hoisted up just that morning,
sipping anisette, & making sure to ignore what was going on

below: some troublesome radical who looked a bit
like a ballerina was letting her toes touch the ground,

pirouetting around that dark & dirty square as if
she loved it — which was truly inexplicable.

Ahem said the guards when anyone lingered too long
With their nose in a posy & then came the stuttered
Explanation was required if one seemed to be admiring
Anything could provoke a ticket even a certain glazing
Of the eye that seemed to signify some secret rapture
How the rupture between looking & *looking* had happened
Was a mystery (perhaps there had once been a sallow queen)
But it was best to wear dark sunglasses & mutter what a waste
Of marble when in the proximity of beauty even when it was
Necessary acts of loveliness such as trimming the olive trees
Were scheduled for Non-Moon nights so the silvery branches
In piles around the ladders wouldn't have any added
Attraction between young men & women was now a case
Of smuggled petticoats & plain brown cakes that had
Icing on the inside & in the schoolyard children traded
Beauty Cards listing what page & book to look in for something
Scandalous things had happened in a town up north it was
Rumored that all the pretty girls had pranced down a cobbled
Hill holding gold picture frames around their faces & a man
With a cane began surreptitiously tracing where the sun was
Hitting the stones & then the mayor whispered *that line* of
Shakespeare into his wife's ear & she looked momentarily
Sentimental outbreaks were not uncommon & there were crews
Trained in containment but they could never predict the next
One day they'd come upon a soda fountain each customer looking
At his or her fizzy drink with an expression of absolute bliss
Or two boys in a basement in ecstasy over something imaginary
Which couldn't be taken away & poured down the sink

THERMAE

I don't have a bath every day. The water bites into you, and as the days go by, your heart turns to water. —PETRONIUS

I. VESTIBULUM *(entrance hall)*

Because he is thinking so hard about his ode, because his mind is full of *what if I fail, what if I can't imagine it* he doesn't notice the man with the ill-fitting toga in front of him whom he would have mocked at dinner — twisting his napkin around his fingers to demonstrate — or the man lurking in a portico, clearly a thief, watching the lines of people fingering their fee. The wait does not seem long to him. Usually he would be peering up at the frescos, trying to let their brightness into him — he'd be dizzy by the time it came to pay — but because now he is trying to reconcile *naval battle* and *just for show*, he barely notices when it's his turn and the attendant has to take the gold coin from him.

II. APODYTERIUM *(dressing room)*

Constellations in the corners. Having unwound their masters' togas the servants hold the wide white circles out in front of their bodies — their dark heads like planets revolving around a moon. Then they fold the moon. Someone here must have seen one of the Naumachiae he thinks as he slips off his tunic, winds his belt around it, and stows the unwieldy scroll. Since he has to worry about it being stolen, he's wearing the wine-stained one, frayed at the hem with an occasional hole. This is not how he dresses for Fortunata who spends two hours each morning fussing with her hair. It was her idea that he come here today, but so far inspiration has not struck. He studies the men's foreheads trying to see waves in the wrinkles, sun-glints and boats in the flecks of their eyes.

III. PALAESTRA *(athletics room)*

O fickle muse, feather ball tossed between men, you come when you want to and never for long. Three men are playing at it, hitting the ball with their palms, softly, as if they don't really want to push it away. Its slow floating is a form of gloating. The arcs their arms make in the air look like entranceways, but their tunics stick to their chests. The ball falls to the floor, a servant picks it up, they begin again. Others roll silver hoops and run after them. The wrestlers require no intermediaries. Naked but for a film of wax and dust, they flex their muscles and slip around like fish, grinding dirt into the bright mosaic floor. If it were that easy. If you could wrestle it down.

IV. LACONICUM *(sweating room)*

Steam makes a dream-scene out of the sweating men. He doesn't know if what beads on his skin comes from in him or from the air. What he does know: sometimes they would flood an existing arena, sometimes they built a lake especially for the battle. Sea animals were put in the water to make it more real. Eels definitely. Surely no sharks. He'd like to include a narwhal, its spiral tusk an element of chance in the planned choreography, but he's not sure his patron will agree. Should he stick to facts when he has so few? Scent of olive oil and musk in the air, servants scraping their masters' skin with strigils until told to stop. He rubs his back against a marble wall.

V. Calidarium *(hot room)*

He will focus on a woman. Always a good idea. Where shall she sit? In the first row of seats, water lapping below her feet. Maybe she sips from a green goblet, makes the scene even stranger by looking through it and cheering for the most wildly-tinted men. Predictably her lover favors the Athenians. She doesn't mind the blood, has seen it all before, but she enjoyed the lion eating the ostrich more. No. Odes should exalt. Begin again. Perhaps she is Fortunata minus the moles, less likely to lecture. Mentally, he gives her the same pretty nose, a few extra charms, then goes to the bronze basin in the middle of the room, splashes scalding water onto his face and arms. For the more modest there are separate baths along the walls. Studying them he decides to use stanzas.

VI. Tepidarium *(warm room)*

With his toe he traces the arabesques from the walls onto the bottom of the bath. Here, everyone is the same height, a head above water, their bodies gangly shadows below. This would be the time to ask someone: A man falls from his replica-ship and drowns. Is he dead then or only when the drama is over — the arena drained and he's found pale and bloated on the floor? It is hard enough to imagine the furnaces beneath the bath — people fanning them, feeding them — or the network of aqueducts criss-crossing the countryside to bring water to this particular silver spout, let alone trying to puzzle out what the eye sees when told *this is the battle* but knows it's not. To him similes seem more scrupulous. Aqueducts act like ideas, but not exactly.

VII. FRIGIDARIUM *(cold room)*

Rain comes in through the oculus making a splashing circle the swimmers avoid. Without the sun the hall is very dark, very cold. He considers not getting in, but his only alternative is to walk home in the wet. From here he can see part-way into the unctuarium — an oiled body shakes under a masseuse's pummeling. Another is picking a perfume. These are the men who will be wrapped in silk, escorted to their litters, carried away without their feet ever touching the streets. He shivers, jumps in, starts swimming. When his fingers hit the pool-end he surfaces. His hair, brown and curly before, is sleek. Squint and he might be the figure he will describe at the start of his poem — Triton, man from the waist up, fish from the waist down, a heart that can't tell the difference.

Lessons in Seeing

1. Examination

The child studies the E in its various
Positions herself squarely on the chair and says
With an air of certainty *comb coming down*
Comb going up and two kinds of comb
Distracted the optometrist fusses with different lenses
And reaches behind her to stop the machine's
Humming he measures her head her eyes and the space
Between her braids her white parting looks like a chalk
Path carved out of a brown hill in the part of England
He grew up in is a hill with a huge naked man carved into
It took a long time to climb up he remembers swaying
Faintly it was a long way down choosing a piece of chalk
Holding it against the fields it spanned five of them including
Sheep were now dabs of white he breathed in *near* and out
Far this is not the tale he tells of how he chose this line
Of work little can be said that anyone will bother to really
Follow the light he says to the girl her lashes flitter her
Pupils shrink into themselves as do people sometimes
When presented with a pair of glasses that give newfound
Clarity is for reading not for seeing a painter once sternly said
To him this does not seem like blasphemy he prefers the children
Who ask why the trees don't flicker red in the fall like they did
Before he can show the girl his pair of glasses that filter out
All the blue in the world his assistant ushers her away and
Brings in an older man who stumbles over the letters A umm D
T B V muttering *why don't these damn things ever form a word*

2. Trompe L'Oeil

This project is to copy a carpet they are giving away because
Its threads are showing she now specializes in what goes
On the floor quite the opposite of magic flying carpets these
Refuse to budge which is a quality highly valued in
Certain circles like to improve on the original idea
She had was to transform concrete walls into airy windows
And marble columns which worked in her apartment but adds
Less to houses with glossy wood floors and real fireplaces
They want something else they want what they already have
Made invincible though they will not step on but around it
When it is done and dry it becomes theirs but sometimes
The family has not yet moved in and she works alone in
Rooms her only spectators forms of furniture vague under
White sheets wrapped paintings leaning against ladders
She waits until the last workman has gone home
In the dark she draws the curtains open places
Six fringed lamps around the sanded rectangle that awaits
Her paints vary imperceptibly though to her they are as different
As a cornflower in a park in Toulon and a cornflower in Michigan
Which is three grades lighter than the lake it sways next
To decide where the shadows should fall she imagines what
Is missing from this room pictures a spiky yucca in
The corner tasseled ropes cinching each curtain at its waist
Slanting light filled with the dust of velvet divans with
These images she overlays the patterns of the carpet so that
It tells two stories this is what it means to fool the eye to
Fool the eye into seeing what is there behind and beyond

3. RESTORATION

Most people would not know where to begin with such a
Mess for him though is like sifting for meaning in
The Bible he finds under one turned-over pew is pristine
The pages uncrumpled not a single corner marked to guide
The reader in times of need and this he finds sadder than
The tiny shattered rose window or the grooves in the floor
Where a heavy saint was dragged away probably years and
Years ago someone lived here he finds a blanket and tin cans
In the confessional spiders have spun beautiful unpenitent
Webs which make him hesitate for a moment his hand on
The brush seems to know where dust and water have made mud
And reveals panels inlaid with shells and enamel he does not
Know what combination of sand and sea smoothed them into
Being far from home did someone select these pink and whites
To bring back and glue to the wall as if to catch the sound
Of crashing waves the priest thinks about how faith hits
Some people from the nearby town have come to look
Through the window they see him tracing the walls like
A blind man and they turn away and walk into
The forest lets little sunlight inside the trees have taken the bell
That fell to the floor into their roots and are golder for
It is twilight when he decides to stop it is only because
He has sanded part of one pew down to the original wood
And found the grain the imperfections the lines to follow

GRADATIONS OF BLUE

The scent of pig is faint tonight
as the lime trees hang their heads against gradations of blue,

looking at the lone suitcase in the middle of the farmyard
with a sense of solidarity. Also forgotten.

Its owner never once looked up at them and exclaimed
I was still soft-fingered when I planted you.

In the plane, her gaze rests on a flock of cloud-birds,
pinkish purple with elongated necks, rests

on the plane's wing-tip colored pink by the sun.
Her head is heavy with this childhood cargo,

like the hawk that usually flies between or above their branches,
found skimming the ground with its catch of mouse or mole,

or the barge that passes every day at four, its metal nose
just out of the water, while empty at eight, its sleek sides

flash signals to those on shore. Later, on the highway
a row of trucks lit like orange squares in the setting sun —

a colony of ants each with a piece of chrysanthemum
on their backs — begins to reassemble memories;

the petals become lining, the shape of the flower is lost,
so that years later, looking at an old photograph,

she will not remember the names of cousins and uncles
but the exact bend in the river behind them, the pattern of trees.

Letting Go

The first time he saw a bell do a full somersault
Against the sky everything afterwards felt too
Flat on his back during break he saw clouds
Regardless of whether his eyes were open or
Not the geese on the pond below nor the plants
Around it reflected his new perspective he expected
Them to swim at a slant or to detect a dizziness in
The daisies were partly covered by a late snow but
Their yellow centers shone through like bells in
Fog mutes the pealing but can't completely conceal
It made sense to him the first time he was told that
Bells were made loud so the Lord would listen
Because it did often seem like he wasn't paying any
Attention and discipline and a pair of leather gloves
Were required for beginner's lessons in the tower
Later he went without and got rope burns to show for
This didn't hurt him what did was letting go when
He wanted to hang on and go clanging up into the sky

IV

The Illuminated Manuscript

1. Monoscene

A master illuminator once painted the Holy Virgin
on one side of a lentil and four Wise Men on the other
my father said he added a fourth because there was
some extra room how we loved imagining that lentil
rimmed in gold with tiny figures crossing its surface
it was rumored that the virgin had individual curls
at her neck that one of the wise men hadn't had time
to shave before setting out across the legume

2. Diptych

Five of my hands
would have fit
in my father's one
yet he was better
at painting smaller
I licked my brush
to make its tip
finer got gold
on my tongue
and spit in my paints
it was months
before I could fit
a smile in a face
a coin in a hand
a crow on a fence

The first day we sat
side by side and
worked on halos
he made me trace
his profile like a
landscape paint a sun
rising behind it
then showed me
how to streak the gold
with bits of black
like the ring he gave
my mother *contact*
with the human darkens
the divine he'd say
kicking her under the table

3. MONOSCENE

I thought of writing as painting's poor relation
tried to be charitable when I was mixing stormy
blue with a just a touch of green and my father
next to me droned on in brown ink if I admired
his script at all it was because the drabness sameness
made the paintings above seem all the brighter
one Sunday he whispered to me *look at the people*
in their pews see how their slant is similar
the preacher began a prayer, we bowed our heads
but a loop of hair or longer line makes all the difference

4. TRIPTYCH

Necessary	writing	tools
Quill	Pounce Pot	Pen Knife
(writing)	(drying)	(correcting)
I	prefer	the
domestic	goose	quill
to	the	wild
for	obvious	reasons
tooth	of	pig
is	optional	can
be	used	to
smooth	the	vellum

5. MONOSCENE

When I showed him my band of red angels a camel
trailed by hoofprints and he said nothing I knew
he was sick he always painted angels in blues and
whites hated the red in the face variety he never
sweated over his work why should they
precision was everything once we spent a whole morning
arguing over the number of humps on a dromedary
he banged his fist twice on the table I pocked the sand
with unresearched hoofprints waited for a reaction
his eyes seemed to follow them over the hill

6. DIPTYCH

Light comes in from the left	*more color less color*
mind the folds where does satin	*catch the shadows*
what about a crease in the velvet	*it is never that smooth*
put some expression on	*his face anger surprise*
why only two stars	*in an entire night sky*
next I shall have you	*paint Judas*

7. MONOSCENE

I page through the book
he was working on
no shoulder blocking
my view of his scrubby trees
skies crammed with rows
of gold stars and his signature
scenes dimly lit back rooms
staircases leading nowhere

not even the last picture
he completed shows any trace
of trembling he knew when to stop
the last two pages have dotted lines
pricked with pins to guide
the writing lightly drawn
outlines of figures showing me
what to fill in not how
my mother says over
and over *the ink will run*
twisting the ring on her finger

IMAGE CAST BY A BODY INTERCEPTING LIGHT

Shadows simplify — the beak combing the back is lost
  in the outlines of the body, the outstretched wing
a sharp shape, featherless, against next-door's brick.
  The light hits so that the shadow birds on shadow wire
slant diagonally while their more creaturely counterparts perch
  on a prim perpendicular. Dreams refract and flatten
this way, changing the postman into "the one who will deliver,"
  letting a lover repent, but in a silly suit in the supermarket.
Ambition also — a man plans his fruit orchards, discovers too late
  he owns acres of rock. It isn't the light that sets him to
tunneling, it's revision of sorts. Now he imagines his groves in
  caves where he can control the sunlight through skylights,
direct one ray at each ripening fruit. Lemons, oranges, limes,
  they flourish down there, nourished below by what would
have gnarled them above. Picture him strolling proudly overhead,
  watching his shadow slipping in between the trees. How could
it not please him to see another figure there, following his footsteps
  inexactly? He begins to think of marriage, of children filling
the caverns with laughter and perhaps for one moment he considers
  the order of creation — that God made the sun and made us after.

 wallowing in it.
ed into gold rolls
ves in concentric circles?
in the fence pulled out
es the papery poppies
 of a foot & hence
, but that's no reason
 or throw out the wedding cakes
 said when a semi spills
river has a choice:

flamingo on the salt flats or *canary in the mines.*
I want the former. I've waited years for the xerox flash
& still no inkling. Lately I've been thinking you
love the groves & don't know how to tell us.
I think you made the steps slick for a reason.

(almost anything)

Dear dust-ghost, the instructions don't make
sense unless I sing them. If the bottom-most hem
is six feet from the ground, how do I get into this dress?
Bird Ode: Dark triangle feet in a wind-field.
Fifth Museum Poem: O swim on through.
Handsome & Then Some: Hello. Please help.
Or if pretending isn't the way, tell me that
the pony's bones are still too soft to hold me
up & take away my paper lantern. Like most
cadenzas I need something to come back to.
I push the rubble out of the second-storey window.
I put the money in an envelope & it's sucked up
a transparent tube. Only the rusted bits of roof

stand out against the sky. Yellow water
in the gutters — always the fault falls somewhere.

(aquatint)

I too am attracted to want, that glass-
bottomed boat, but there are some things
you could have told me: the forest of shiny black
mussels did not cut my feet. As for the oysters,
this is where the beak took them. This is where
they cracked. Inventing the propeller only blurred
the picture. I know my options — anemones sting
whatever they think is prey. Me, I'm planting
forget-me-nots by the ziggurat, pulling out
all the gorse. I didn't see the clamshells skid
along the beach, but I can study the pattern.
I think a horse was here. Amaze me with
what you know. Do the barnacles really look
like ancient daisies, did the starfish really
turn orange & purple from holding on?

(good-bye to if)

The plastic pagoda hasn't helped nor have
the pills. Red to green, no sign of yellow.
There's no way to know if you're listening.
Why does two always have to be a tawdry,
fluttering thing? Throw it to the side of the road
& find some other canvas. Let the statues
soften, my hand shadow itself for a change.
Throw your light on the bricks or the cracks
in-between, it won't impress the invalids in
hammocks taking their pulses. They know how

to count. Slice through the bleating & you have
six pairs of smallish gloves, pearls at each wrist.
No one said anything about violet-water or later.
The next time a rhinestone falls to the floor,
you won't find me on my knees.

(magnet mine)

It isn't a question of what's quaint, what
hurts. If the telephone wires look like
an endless perch, the birds will avoid
the trees. The train's reflection in the water
can't help but glimmer more than the train.
As long as the local cathedral has an
unpronounceable name, people will come in
droves to sing their songs to the residual blue.
When rain was wanted they used to shoot
cannonballs into the clouds. So prosaic. So pretty.
The planets couldn't be more so. Or if it's scale
that attracts you, come closer — there are seven
tiny piles of bright pigment in the sink. Lava-less-
lament, flimsy-attempt-to-draw-you-in —
call them what you want, but call them.

(thin trumpet)

Sweet triple trochee, finite font of counsel,
must you always be a swan in the distance?
I try to cut through the water & end up
circling away like a fly shy of its shadow.
I hold you up but all around me are higher things.
Throw me in with the crows trying to untie
the yellow bows on garbage bags with their beaks.

This time I'll take the long route to the dovecotes —
it'll ease things if they're empty. Yes,
it's unnecessary, but how was I to know
that a lover would be just another blank sky?
In a fever I felt something once, so here I am,
still collecting glimpses, standing on the edge
of the dock. I am standing on tiptoe. My eyes
are closed. Throw an arrow at my eyelids.

(always the body)

Every dog is mad & straining at its leash.
The trees in the water have turned white,
lost all their leaves. Flood plain in the middle
of the forest, my mismatched bouquet, how
does it all fit together? I don't have the others'
oracular bones, am tentative in stairwells,
in corridors, in general. The soap won't melt
for me. In the marble factory, they're making
every type of torso with neck-sockets so
they can add the heads later. I'm assuming you
took into consideration that ghost-prints can't know
original ink, that lacquering watercolors smears them.
For your information, the view from here is less
than stellar. I don't remember yesterday or tomorrow.
Tell me: who slips next, who swallows the stone?

(sum of glimpses)

Constant corrector, make the unusual choice.
It is all spoiled by speaking too soon.
Pry me away from the undersides of bathtubs,
people with strange names & the oh so occasional
insight. Someone is crying in another room.

60

Never again such soft light, never again
this alluvial soil. What defense is there?
I lick the four black corners, press them
onto the page & still the photograph slips
out. My spine in the x-ray — chandelier
under water, scribbled genie in a bottle.
I want to believe this is why we swerve because
certainly it's not the heart that holds us up.
Someone is painting a still life of peaches &
kerosene. Someone is lining the grottos with glass.

(bottle tower)

Dear nine-thirty: is there any word
for the way the peony blossoms bend over
& rest their soft faces on the petals piled up
in the grass? Tar cools & tires dull you.
The puddles are milky & grey. There are
daughters who die before their mothers, men
mute with mistakes, birds with broken necks
stuck to the sidewalk. The woodpile is full
of the blank faces of owls. Today I want to live
without looking. Give me that & I will give up
the rest. Fat green buds bursting to split into
pink. Trucks piled high with glittering tar.
The way the rain makes the ground give up
its heat so that I feel it at my knees &
the grass starts to smell like the sea.

(across the mouth)

Absent gauze over my gaze, aren't you
even going to try & translate? The river

is brimming too. They're finding fish in
the playground. Or shall I start with something
less literal, inward whistle, bookshelves with
doors. I never did learn the tongue-tied limpid-eyed
way to implore, kept tripping over solutions.
When I first tried to copy a painting, I bought
the requisite red pencil for forty-four cents,
pressed it to paper. I wasn't looking to be
surprised, though I'd sooner call my lover
snowy plover than some little brown bird.
When it all crashes, I want to know what to do
with the shards of green. What if I can't
separate white from sugar from snow?

(bas-relief)

It's a foolish place to be in, groping
around on the floor waiting for
the spider to fall. I encounter only cracked &
blackened fruit, illegible newspapers.
In your carnival of intervals I am always last.
This was the obvious place to come to.
In the store-window, the wood is stained
green where the fish was. I'm the creaturely
one with saucer eyes examining the dab of lime
at the tip of each brown twig. The cars on the wet
road sound like scissors cutting cloth. I've always
found it easier to leave people who make no sound
when they breathe. Won't you stand out? Can you really
condemn us for liking to watch each other eating cake,
for secretly thinking unbecoming is a beautiful idea?

(obscure choir)

I can't be coy after all I've done. Today
the clouds aren't letting anything through.
The soprano faints rather than hitting that highest
note. Always under the apse, whatever it's made of,
hopelessly hoping for rain — there are the days I forget
& don't think of you once, emerge from the changing room
in what I was wearing before. Or I stay in bed,
lousy with sleep, lousy with love, where I meet
only unwilling messengers. Excess of love:
I have one extra bottle of orange syrup. Please
tell me where I should send it. Excess of desire:
seven petticoats in the moat. Though my hands
stick to everything, I can't place the cricket's call.
I'm sorry. I don't mean to be all mouth
when already so many roar in your name.

(silver print)

The lock sticks again. I can make a self-
portrait out of anything. My silhouette
in the window is all elbows. Blossom to stem —
the rust roses on the pipes are blooming
backwards. The head pushes its way out,
learns how to waver later. Upside-down
in the spoon, I think I am getting closer —
second-hand skimming time, blue windows
everywhere, sharp smell of keys in the air.
Where are you inevitable slap? I have propped
the storm windows against the side of the house
for you: twenty paintings of the sky & five grills

heaped with charcoal so the air above them
shimmers, shatters. Tell me I'm not just forging
a copy, tell me you're more than the moon.

(whitewash)

Maybe it *is* all a game. The chairs don't seem
to touch the stage. My shoes make too much
sound. I have a friend who is always
checking her pockets. Maybe I should pick
a trinket & leave it at that, take back the invisible
reins. I hate the thought of it. All those useless
lists: an interloper to string the lights onto please.
Someone in a similar muddle. Wasps hang in the air.
Like question marks? No. The pigeon is random,
not a sign. The perfume drifts from another
neck. Even with each tuning peg twisted
tight, I can't bear people's knowing
looks. This murk has nothing in common
with silver altars, gold thread. Who put
the canopy in my head? I can't see past it.

(horror vacui)

I would have liked an answer.
In the abandoned orangery, caterpillars
have chewed constellations from the leaves.
In the picture I look like part of the gate.
The crows with their nib-like beaks stay
outside like all lacunae, watching dust
sift slowly onto the river. Each time I step
forward the starlings scatter, despite the gentle

diagonals I choose, my indifferent mouth.
The experiment with sand & violin
failed, no music emerged, no voice was
conjured up. I've been dreaming in duplicate
but we have nothing in common. I know now
how to kneel, that's all. I wasn't just another
worn coin. I would have liked an answer.

ONE FILAMENT AGAINST THE FIRMAMENT

Most days Group V. practiced on seeing through
Prisms because of the way they bend the light
They are considered the first marker of advanced
Sight tests had been conducted on them all as
Children these ones could examine a dewdrop
Perched on a furred leaf & not cry when it fell to
The ground had no more data to give though later
The books would be buried to give us something new
To discover God could not be a matter of spaceships
The way must be found through the mind &
The eyes are distractible as the Leader discovered one night
In a stairwell when one lightbulb overhead managed
To distract him from the sky outside he decided
That finding beauty pointless might actually be the
Point at something & then see past it became
The first lesson to lessen attachment to things put
Here to distract us of course there were detractors
Who thought the fingers or tongue would work just
Fine lines of personality scar the fingertips though
& tastebuds cannot belie their bias only the mind
& the eyes could absorb indefinitely pupils practiced
Not shrinking at the sun it was an honor to go blind
Trying to ignore the tiny creatures that float across
Our eyes was a task that drove hundreds crazy because
It didn't make sense that something tiny & see-through
Could lure the gaze away from the Taj Majal or a Monet
Which they practiced in front of because of the lovely
Colors & affection for them were eliminated later as were
All forms of luxury like being able to see your family
Across the breakfast table they all disappeared one by
One day everybody woke up alone & couldn't find
Each other & they all would have died from standing

Still there was one girl who hadn't been able to stop loving
The word marshmallow & one boy who still had a favorite
Color slowly seeped back into the world & a new group
Formed to research why it had left but it never became clear

About the Author

Matthea Harvey holds an M.F.A. from the University of Iowa's Writers' Workshop. She serves as Managing Editor for *American Letters & Commentary* and a poetry editor for *Boston Review*. She lives in New York City.

Alice James Books has been publishing exclusively poetry since 1973. One of the few presses in the country that is run collectively, the cooperative selects manuscripts for publication through both regional and national annual competitions. New authors become active members of the cooperative, participating in the editorial decisions of the press. The press, which places an emphasis on publishing women poets, was named for Alice James, sister of William and Henry, whose gift for writing was ignored and whose fine journal did not appear in print until after her death.

Typeset and designed by Lisa Clark
Printing by Thomson-Shore

RECENT TITLES FROM ALICE JAMES BOOKS